I

WANT

YOU

TO

TELL

ME

A

STORY

ABOUT

UNKNOWING

ME

EVEN

THE

MIRRORS

HAVE

BECOME

BARS

WE

LEAN

AGAINST

GEPHYROMANIA

TC TOLBERT

NIGHTBOAT BOOKS
NEW YORK

Gephyromania was first published by Ahsahta Press in 2014.

ISBN: 978-1-643-62120-3

Cover design by Quemadura
Cover artwork: Tomiko Jones, 40°40'N 121°63'W River Wash,
Mount Hood, Oregon, from "Landscapes"
Book design by Janet Holmes

CATALOGING-IN-PUBLICATION DATA
is available from the Library of Congress

Nightboat Books
New York
www.nightboat.org

CONTENTS

Gephyromania | 1

    (ir)Retrieval | 17

    What Space Faith Can Occupy | 24

    elegy | 25

    On braiding hair already cut away from the scalp | 26

    A Love Note for My Breasts | 28

    The Trapping Sessions: (Free) | 29

    Offering | 31

    Testing . . . | 32

    Tau(gh)t | 33

    shoulder gratitude | 39

    Thaw | 40

territories of folding | 45

    Crossing | 53

    latitude: [perceived obsolescence]: unplanned | 54

    Underneath February is a test strip. And believe me. Believe me.
      I would. | 57

    The Palinode | 58

    Spending Log | 61

    On Minimalization | 62

    From *Passing* . . . | 64

A Congress of Bring and of Invisible: The Language of Heaven
  is No | 67
The exit signs are behind us. | 70
Beg Approval | 71

Gephyromania | 79

Bridges I am thankful to have crossed | 93

Bridges over troubled water | 97

about the author | 99

GEPHYROMANIA

All we are is representation, what we appear to be & are, & are not.

Larry Levis

decorate almost, queer

      miscreant

                                  (bear some boy)

and sing

To remove from the frame of
reference the referent. To erase
singular.   (and plural.)   and yet.
The verb never agrees
with its heresy. Disbelieving.
In absentia. We dress.

The story of cleavage unwritten.
Erased.   (perhaps.)   but still missed.

You who chose to sidle through the window. In a body no longer possible still a when. Please, still a when, please gently. Least lately, double saunter, through the rest.

She said the thing I want to remember is the leave-taking.
Do not break me
and I promise not to not let the seam down.
Do not stand there.
Toes sewn together and thrown.

ev-er-y skin   with a would may
if   awillisthis

I believe too much in repetition.

(grafting an exegesis of skin)

(who will I ask and under what influence)

(if this is the fate of familial)

(Suddenly Seymore and here's a fish in your hand)

(what the mouth covers and in covering, regrets)

And yet. We are a bedrock of antecedents.

(& sing. & sing.

& sing.)

I always mistook my face for less sinister. I have only one secret and in forty seconds that number will become less than three. When I wash dishes, I fill up the largest bowl with water, soap, and silverware. I place this large bowl in the chest of the sink. Notice the rule of nonrecollection. It is paramount to the myth of the sink.

Only the fact of what I was thinking there can separate me. Less than a decade but what the sink said was *years*. Can someone please pass me the Technicolor. Having lived through the funnel both ways. Little intuition calls the scene.

spurious, concomital, and

loverly

she's a good boy
no matter what he's

both tired of the obvious and
invigorate arrive in us holyfield arrive
a girder we fashion from our teeth

I do not bring the luxury of insistence.
If a cattle guard is waning I am south.
6 poles. and not a one of them in training.
Although I am ungentle and in between,
dear Ramona. Call me domicile.
Tar string and say that never will you
garnish me. Choke lovely the open
trickle of my mouth.

no^{...}

(boy, oh boy, and sing.)

In this, they encourage disparation. One is pressed quietly between the welcome where two sets of bars strain to meet. Do not hold your hands like a lift to me. They are given twice as empty as sound.

To stand between the text and its articulation. Pin through a simple semblance of consistency. The button eye punches down a veil.

Would that the ribs flail sullen in the winter. (arbitrary in stasis) given wings. It is hard not to say what we are missing. (if found uncovering   waying   driven bring) A topiary digressing in the mouth.

That there will be a future

in which   my twinkle

toes   calibrate rescue

(finger the witness lightly now lightly)*

in the salty and discontinuous air

*as if that woman I was still asleep in her jeans

Because I left words out I did not want to repeat in the winter.

Leaning, as if on wind.

(what water holds.)

You move forward as if through a jump rope.
The handles molesting your hands.

What the mouth covers, and in covering, introduces.

We keep a tidy coroner of yesterday's wind.

Ir]Retrieval

That _____ was born Melissa Dawn Tolbert, December 24, 1974
to a woman named Jeanne Darline. That in this
we decorate almost. We mean (*we relegate*) we mean.
That the hopeful bearded face becomes a tyranny.
(That what we believe in is a form of refraction. The back turning
as a word, upon itself. Draping the neck into sound.) That there lies
a calloused form of predicate beneath the Rupaul.
That the body which is her body is a decency.
That we draw can(n)ons around permissible and rest.
That a book I received I then decided to return to you.
That I do not know forgiveness for the things we choose to leave.
That, like the afterimage given to a closed eye.
She is prologue. And simultaneous. She is domicile.
That this is not therefore. (*salient*.) That she bring.

She remembers that there are names, kinder names,
for the accidental bruising left by witness. And
sedulous in her canter these are illegible. With a mouth
full of tinder. and forget. With a hand, not a shade,
and a gleaning. That she may liquefy all outposts. and fall back.
That there is a causal born predisposed to a reachliness.
That there are fists with which my mouth has not met.
In what became known as *The Topography*
of Unrequited Laughter, You Fucking Suck, and *The Pedagogue*
of Sixth and Silhouette. It is not so much that transferable
is in the offering. (Although I am ungentle and
in between, dear Ramona.) That you come home
anyway. And bring the telephone of your liking.
That you block discreetly and settle spring between my mouth.

That we are a history. On a good day. A context. The path
of a paper airplane drawn optimistically about the edges
of a room. That my hands do still so little (grieving)
to listen to me. Usurpers of sleep and yet
their genius is temerity. That they memory
they memory they member. (non-consensual.) They member
they memory they rest. In this, they encourage
disparation. They gentle Hustler, Man 2 Man,
and Too Deep. (we are patching this in on film.)
That the bathroom is guileless in its obscurity. What we
reach for when placing a _____ in the mouth.
Do not hold your hands like a lift to me.
Lying just below the derivative of undertow. That they
are given twice as empty as sound.

It's not silence I'm afraid of, it's commodification.

(on peeing on, seeing on, *Out.*)

Masturbation's just not the same without menstruation: what
with all the delectable injectables: where what's obscure
outweighs antiquity: to obdurate cheekily: there's little
that's been improved here: he's in and, clearly, she's out.

Faux hawk   ☑   (:when it all comes down to hegemony)

Chin stache   ☑   (: i.e. and/or even the pathology of and/or)

White speak   ☑   (: gephyromania is interminable and dis-ease)

Ellipses   ☑   (make that a double check) (: with regard to virile mangos,
friends, and (more important) money: the subtextual consciousness of queer.)

I press curiously tender to your Arabia. (oh baby i)

My labia swell and Really. That's so neat and all.

But it's the rise of the dicklet we all cheer.

disappearing wheelbarrow, I wish you wheelbarrow.
the whiskey rash reel off the hand.
the ballyhorse leg is a spoonfall; applesauce
class in a round. hermeneutically sealed
in a braindrop (we are) fucking shit up
with insistence. the barrel chain bounty gives
ground.   Mercedes! Mercedes! Despite the genuflect.
how much plow could really you land in a day.
despite the eyelids and the pants that fall
accordingly. despite Rothko, repatriation,
and the parallel. what will generous make
broken in the handoff. (we are) (tiny) a population
of peligro. despite the temperature and armistice of when.
(we are) rebar: for rent or for rain.

(So that there is at least one flag you will never know the weight of.)

(So that the chair has many permutations.)

(So that you move forward as if through a jump-rope.
The handles molesting your hands.)

(So that there are peepholes in which we are still lingering.)

(So that my tits are still tits in the summertime.)

(So that as long as I hold you I will continue to pour my hair out.)

(So that lack may not measure thickness, nor health, nor sound.)

That the body which is my body is a relevancy.
That the new body which is irrelevant is a test.
That there's never been a man in the room. That,
were it not for one man fucking me back into existence,
I would have sworn to you that I thought I saw two.
That there are now tears in what was supposed to be
impermeable. That either way I am unable to be conceived.
That the body which is my body is indeterminately.
That there is little room for the tiny tufts of toilet paper.
That I will hold them in the verisimilitude I continuously
refer to as my chest. That this is somehow a demonstration
of bravery. That better models of logic are exemplified
by this drain. That erosion is why some still believe in philanthropy.
That this is a prayer shawl. That still we refuse to call her by her name.

WHAT SPACE FAITH CAN OCCUPY

I believe that witness is a magnitude of vulnerability.
That when I say love what I mean is not a feeling
nor a promise of a feeling. I believe in attention.
My love for you is a monolith of try.

The woman I love pays an inordinate amount
of attention to large and small objects. She is not
described by anything. Because I could not mean anything else,
she knows exactly what I mean.

Once upon a time a line saw itself
clear to its end. I have seen the shape
of happiness. ($y=mx+b$)
I am holding it. It is your hand.

ELEGY

I am so not myself (sometimes) I look at her.
And we are never equal to the break that we bring.

ON BRAIDING HAIR
ALREADY CUT AWAY FROM THE SCALP

let there be silence. and plenty.
let there be end tables. breasts. buoys.
let there be exit ramps. breasts. balls.

when what essentially I made off with was your stair.
like a tunnel grieves a view of the sky:
all the emptiness between my teeth is a gift.

pray down the mirror our reflection says we
see through. your new lover on one side of the street.
your new bicycle. and then, therefore, you.

pray down a rope around the syllable
that haunts us. the narrative that continually takes
itself too seriously. a symphony of strangulated rests.

our music undone periscopically.
the pornography remains inexhaustible.
a white flag fading at the root.

and what void can we still find our way into.
victimless.
a hand signaling daylight to the sky.

a myelin mouth frozen open in the bedroom.
what you recognize is not me, is (not) me.
that, inside the body which is not your body

to defibrillate, your plastic hands articulate a bruise.
(I love you more with your pants down.) pray down an overpass.
because a demonstrative is lingering in the airway.

all pedal and unfrozen—will you see me?
pray down a casino and then a cornfield in the coda.
(prayitdownprayitoverpassmeoverprayitdownpassitoverprayitback)

tooth enamel is the strongest substance in the human body.
shame is not something we carry.
it multiplies in the recesses of our mouths.

because one hand still reaches into the empty.
pray down the pressure of your hand on my body.
a violence of comfort and request.

A LOVE NOTE FOR MY BREASTS
(ABRIDGED)

Thank you for the joke about tuning in. I'm cutting you off now. For my grandmother and the way she talked about my grandfather. She said he liked her for her big brown eyes.

~

Thank you for protecting me from straight women. I'll miss that. For making me think long and hard about why there was a marriage I was leaving. For the 1997 I never had.

~

THE TRAPPING SESSIONS: (FREE)

Somehow,
if I speak the same: (do I speak the same)
negative capability is just a word. (Word.)
I live in that compression. Language—
do something unusual
to languish me. Language me,
language, steal my voice.

Let's just say I'm the
fish. Yes. I'm the fish begging
tricks for less air.
Compositional improv is not metaphor.
My voice changed and I
thought I was k(no)wingly.
Speak memory, speak. _____.
Memory: break voice.

Smile (defer) smile, smile,
shimmy. Wink—wait. That's not *my*
line. My line slipped.

A table covered
with t-shirts is a living
room. And who wouldn't
feel safe in that ray-
o-gram. Where we are only
what the light cannot
prove. (I live in that
compression.) And who wouldn't
language in whose voice.

If there is not here
there's a line I crossed. Somewhere valence
got Prufrocked with the T.

Tell me something porch light
and give it earplugs. I swear to god
my clit's the size of your arm.

You have forgotten that I do so little
with the skin I'm in. You make me a ladder
and now I want you to make me more.

OFFERING

A rope and then somehow it's opposite.
Cantilevered.
An amalgam of pre-injury rests.

TESTING . . .

When in the company of men. Ketchup.
I spilled paint on my leg and now I know
what I want for my next tattoo.

If men are divisible by five.
Rip, rip, rip, rip, rip.
                        Done.

The rectangle colored with squares.
dash of coiled hose. sprig of shadow.
dash again. or pocket change. watch
people.   you.

You're two inches higher than god.
(oops, floppy. staple, pin, sew, clasp, copy
erase erase erase

better.)

Son?

TAU(GH)T

I go back to that no and I sing from it.
I practice epilogue: needlethreadepi-
thelium. As what constitutes mean is the
variance. Perhaps I fly hollow. Into
some you, then. And rest. And where will the drama
queen darling? My tongue is thin without your tongue
to build a team on. Because we have been there,
dear Ranger. Let me punt to you. Face first is
the new tyranny of winged-ness. We were
a Jerusalem of avalanches gone
cleanly. Grip the resting heart, wresting. (Love, rest.)

Pre-existential condition: we. Victim-
ized and plural and. I will say you until
I break it. I will say it. Your father
drove while you slid your hand out the window. What
became a roof with no house, just some sky. We
barter what we witness. Because I can for-
give what forgives not forgets. This is a house
on fire. I will say it. You are changing. You
are not never there. And what will shame me in
to breathing if I lose you. And what will pre-
sent tense if not corroborate with the past.

[this will always be the bathroom where I fucked
you where I fuck you where I fuck you where I
pee this fucking goes ongoing fuck with me
fucking you memory by member I re-
member you dick will do that dick will
barter baby's restless call it the blue year
dick will dip you dick will slip you dick will knee
who told you momma may be an omnivore
but she always comes home to eat I got your
gruel right here baby fire me that's what she said
I see fuck too much this fucking fuck with me]

I hesitate to use the phrase palm tree
because palm tree is so Miami. Nonethe-
less. Palm trees are indicative of regret.
When the palm tree does what it is doing now.
A thing anthropomorphic and lovingly
to my back. This happened in Fayetteville once
but, horticulture being what it is, the
palm tree lost by popular vote. There is no-
thing more humiliating than replacement.
To quote Eric Magrane, *I'm not certain why*
(you, me) *we conceived in this order the world.*

Where does coffee enjoy you in your new home?
I am a guest. And as such I will be mis-
taken. The porch chair disintegrated and.
With it the severalties abated. I
cannot say *I miss her*. I can, however,
own up to what I did to the chair. Can you
masturbate? No, never. Memory is use-
less. Still. Her hand was a chronology of
irrevocable. The shape of happiness.
I imagined 4 trillion lost cells inside
it: nevering and the press back of the ear.

And please that we not clobber nor posture. Plead
fists that forget their fists and drive up dumbly
inside. Praise the devil right out of my hands
and pray he leaves hard. Pray a house on fire and
praise the mouth that surely claims it. I say you.
Pray it down. Pray it over. Pray it back. It's
an old story, babe. And I can safely say
I lean on it. Dear so and so. I'm sorry
I brought the megaphone to your calling hours.
Pray blinding. Praise faith without cleaving. Pray pre-
sent tense is not an admission of that theft.

Last night when I looked at you there was a you
looking back and she was dreamy. And by dream-
y I do not mean dream-like but thick. I miss
your shoulders. You know how all wet I get for
all things disparate. The teeth not teeth and did
you cut yourself your hair hidden or the hat.
This peeping on you is irregular but
consistent. In 08, "overshare" was the
new word of the year. If precipitant then.
Then reason says rest. Implicate agent or
agency. Retract. retractretractgenuflect.

Not face never over do not send that. I
called you a whore and I scared. Scared face, do no
over. Scared scared. A body con no not fist
it. A body con not never there. Would you
be my noose? Never darling. Noose you nicely.
Would you lungs on? Breasts on? Never face me? I
called you a whore, you noose, try by me. Never.
Con face scared. Share. A body called fist loose me
tightly. You darling con do not wish me there.
Lungs, will you? (scared) Will you? (whore) Scared. Never. Noose
fist nicely. Never con never loose fist share.

This is a house under fire. Lovely. I will
say you. When I say you my dick hurts. I am
a dick. I am a sex addict. My dick hurts.
When I say you I'm not between. I am hung.
This is a house from fire—say you. I'm not stop
say you. After fire. Nearing fire. Among. I
will say you fire say you until I break you.
Saying you fire playing you I am alone.
Stay stay you not lay you. I am a sex ad-
dict. I am celibate. I am bent over
a fire and I am offering it my lungs.

Thin is tongue wing-ed, not not birds. There been have
wresting heart, resting—gone cleanly. Oh build us
Jerusalem in our tongues, steal us seamly.
Build us out of no build us into first build
the epilogue build the hollow hollow wall.
Tiny bathroom the be will always the be
will dip you and dip you forget not sky. Home.
Cleaving without faith, praise (home) blinding. Praise teeth
not teeth, you can chair. Your to brought sorry am
I so and so, pray I leave hard. Your to were
tyranny, grip the wrestless. build build love (rest)

The body is a tiny pool, a pool one
expects to see the bottom of. The woman
came and went with many different objects in
her mouth. The conclusive shape of happiness
is a triangle. We are mostly not birds.
Confession is the logical opposite
of light. The body is proximity we
mistake for proximity. If the theory
is that misogyny is throat culture. For
people with mothers. I take it back. I have
to give it to you. But, first. I take it back.

SHOULDER GRATITUDE

what was an avalanche played a fawn and did it cleanly.
how I worship your weather. my many mouths and their injuries,
come this way. and this way, and your periphrastic, your handing me row.

please, darling, and the teeth in my nether-regions.

let that it be visible and sooner: the theory of perilous and the pleasure
of a boot coming down. if there was a philosophy of intimate
that could shame you. I holy cleavage. and of subjunctive, I holy this.

THaw

You said I will pull you out of my body in 237
ways. What you wanted was beautifully to
sever things. Here love: the same things. changed.

Finally: a taxonomy of afterthoughts. As though
you were the one who was
sleeping. Breathing in the marrow of would.

You, who are a valley of no, I hear the music leaking. (How she.
How she. How I.) You say *low key* and I do not believe you.
I forgive everything: the perseveration of skin.

My hands that are a chopping block and I
cannot touch him. I cannot touch him
without not touching me.

Because if you leave, and you are already leaving, there are three.
But you say less than three. And the couch, in your absence,
is crenellated. And who is going to watch us as we leave.

To add to the list of changing things: life preservers are no longer
about preservation. They have become less holy. PFD =
personal flotation device. Endlessly possible. Unlike wood.

Stacey May Fowles wants a lover who will hit her.
(I do not believe in submission.) I want you to erase me.
This is a kindness. A kindness you tell me. A kindness I do not deserve.

On the floor. By the bed. Hotel Congress. March 19, 2005.
Room #23. We are a long way from disintegrated. You said *Now*.
Look at me. And I did. And you bloomed.

(*When my mother died,* I will say.
Many years after my mother has died.
But I will not believe her. I'll be like my grandmother who

despite my parade of girlfriends and her profession
that *nobody should be mean to them*, still
doesn't believe in being queer.

I don't believe in being dead,
I'll tell my dead mother. And just like you
she'll repeat herself. *Happy New Year. Happy New Year. Happy New.*)

I expect there will be a morning when you walk up to this very gate
while I am sitting here. I know this. I know you less each time I see you.
I know this like I know you are more lonely than glass.

To your languishing. To your bubbly.
To your recent. To your hologram. To your desperately.
To your seeking. To your dictaphone. To your you.

Neuromuscular facilitation is just another way of saying
Vancouver. Always is yet a matter of roller derby. Just
in love with you. You, more than sleep.

In the top drawer is a photograph of them touching.
It is not so much that it is a photograph.
It is that it is a depiction of what. not could.

I want to tell you about my body. About testosterone
as unwitting art historian. About recovery. Me(n). What it feels like
underneath there. The part you cannot know. but should.

Either way. It's a house. It's a house
like everyone else has. I take things away.
I don't take them for good.

How delirious must we sound when we are falling.
I miss you, you can't even imagine. And how bad
at math. *Less than three. Less than three. Less than three.*

And what if. I completely remember
it wrong. What if I remember there were two
of us. And then what if. there was only one death.

I do not believe in the existence of holes
that lead to nowhere. Muscle memory remains an enigma. Still, you cannot
touch her. You cannot touch her without not touching me.

(And still) you are not not a part of me. The world is
uncharacteristically unresponsive.
I could thank you. You stay with me. like grass.

TErriTORieS OF FOLDinG

We leave to be who we will become. We go back to see who we are.

CD Wright

This cannot be another year about _____ (unknowing). I was my mother's daughter and then a series of days came. They were not unlike a rock garden on the dinner table. I brushed the ground and made a lifejacket of fence posts. We committed suicide and she called me her sum.

Pushed in a closet and bleeding.

If this is 1989:

    your sister did that   to your nose.

sometimes I believe I am a hallway. (I take back the whole part about transitioning.) and this is what I keep trying to tell you about desperation. (if I could I would suffer more in that liminal.) my wish which is a faulty maintaining. the tender of a slightly turned knee. (I am the least brave person that I know.)

It's spelled s-h-e but the s is silent.

Isn't that the way it is anyway. No two plurals in the world.

And what of CPR in the first place.

Play dead, little sister, be a good girl.
I'll be the boy and I'll save you.

This is air in your lungs and you are now
breathing. It is important to me that you
remember the difference. This is
resuscitation. Not blood or a kiss.

CROSSING

When you hold me there are words for that.
I do not remember the words for that but I remember that there are words.
There are not words for when you do not hold me.
I remember that there are no words in the world so I say them.
Abolishing a line is only one way to mark it.
My throat hurts from saying so much nothing.
When I tell you *I love you* what I really mean to ask is *can I change?*

LATITUDE: [PERCEIVED OBSOLESCENCE]: UNPLANNED

(we lay there for months drawing back
tiny muscle. and grafting an exegesis of skin.)

My voice, which is the most terrible gift from me.
Indiscriminately. You refuse to touch me with sound.

I want you to tell me a story about unknowing me.
Even the mirrors have become bars we lean against.
Even the body has become a gift we regret.

Either way, I showed up today with my cast on.
With what I wouldn't give to hear you say *Technicolor*.
With a guitar and an E string that sticks to itself.
With elephants and a memory of what was found.

It is hard to imagine there are fingers
that do not belong to me. That speak a language
to your body I do not know.

Come closer love, and do not diminish me.
These, which are the politics of our nevering
and you, who are a fistful of duet.
Pressed generously in the girders of my back.

It is not so much that we are
unbroken. Standing like a cyclone
on the periphery of that door.

The cataracts of leaving distinguish me.
And yet. I believe in this retrieval. You,
who are an elliptical. a sweeping. a banishment.

Come closer. Rest my hand on that fragile.

Yesterday.

A silence we begin for.

And yesterday.

The crossing nothing ~~comes~~. back.

UNDERNEATH FEBRUARY IS A TEST STRIP.
AND BELIEVE ME. BELIEVE ME. I WOULD.

Men is another moment of happily.
They say *your body*. My breasts
in my hands and. Your hands
cleaving. I said I would tether them.
Lay your hands down—I will
sever them like wood.

THE PALINODE

It is your birthday and you are a beautiful boy. We are beautiful boys
on a motorcycle. You wave to other bikers and the other bikers wave to
the beautiful boys. Beautiful boys on a motorcycle waiting for a train
and your gloved hand reaches for me. We laugh and your gloved hand
reaches me. Your gloved hand and the motorcycle are missing. Your
gloved hand waves to other bikers. Beautiful boys, your birthday is over.
Your gloved hand, beautiful boy. Beautiful boy, your gloved hand. How
beautiful. Beautiful. I'm cold.

~

Part of it is that we are at a gun show.
Part of it is that we are at a gun show
but we have not come together. The danger
of not coming together. Put the gun down, dear
and take the bullets out sweetly. Push them
one by one. Marry them
to the muscle that sits between our bones.

~

Let's just say I remember everything. Eating a ham sandwich for the
first time in your living room. My leather belt and the way you loved
its smell at eye level. Markered up lids of olive jars. The gentle way the
linoleum gave beneath you when you begged your knees into the floor.

(New ending: I am the red-winged monster curled inside you like a fist.
It is not so much the darkness that concerns me. It is the loose thing, the
clambering thing I imagine inhabits your chest.)

~

As of October 21, 2006 I will officially be becoming a new kind of man.

You won't forgive me for taking me away from you.

When, for the last four days I've dreamt about you, I've woken

up close to the ugliest thing I've ever known:

~

I love you and you are out gun shopping.
(Forgive me. For taking me away.)
I love you. You. No longer. So I'm told.

SPENDING LOG

Having been unmade and then

made again by the eyes

of white men What

I have passed in order to be in gendered

Erased and still under scored Repeat

Failure is a practice

of the living Somehow I am

always in LA looking back at a billboard

A count of change is not the same as

paying the cost Why transition if not to

unlearn how the eye was

trained to work on the world

ON MINIMALIZATION
(AND ON THE MORE DISCREET NOTION OF RISK.)

Do not look at sentences sideways. Do not insert commas where periods are sufficient. Do not elucidate, subjunctive, or retract. Do not nickname. Above all, do not nickname yourself. Do not abbreviate when what you want is an intimacy. Do not whisper to the sister with whom you share a small bed. Do not share a small bed. Do not sleep deeply enough that you wander from the house.

Do not wear a face that says precious. Do not be anti-precious. Be sincere but not overly-so. Do not be aggressively sincere. Do not be a girl who plays softball. Do not play softball and do not hang out with other girls. Do not be a girl who curls her eyelashes. Do not love to see how she would look if she were bound. Do not love eyelash curlers. Do not love bondage. Know that other girls can see you. Know that they may be tempted to feel betrayed. Do not be a girl. Do not love the bondage of being a girl. Do not be tempted. Do not feel betrayed.

Do not believe in hell more than you believe in other things. Do not discover masturbation in the 3rd grade. Do not masturbate. Do not ask god to strike you with diarrhea or stomach pain. Do not believe in alcoholism, vegetarianism, or tongues. Do not cry nor practice *fuck* with your mouth. Do not shower in the house alone. Do not shower at night. Do not lock the door but always close it. Do not yell at anyone who enters because this may anger them and they may become suspicious. Do not make a spectacle of your struggling. Do not hide yourself but do not pick a fight.

Interrogate any pleasure relentlessly. Do not participate. You may find casual encounters to be the most obscene. Do not count the telephone poles as you pass them. Do not imagine you are a table saw. And then a wash. Then a crowd. Do not smoke cigarettes at a young age. Do not practice smoking cigarettes at a young age. Behind a locked door in the bathroom at the mirror. Do not fixate orally. Do not look at yourself. Do not remember you have a jealous hole for a mouth.

I believe a line set down
at any point in space is
infinite. The body is a collection
of linear.   Crepuscular.   Dumb.

If I believed in little arrows
shooting off the end of every i
I'd be asking for it.
          I'd be taking over.

The body doesn't need that.
The body is retractable.

Touch me.
          We'll become less one.

I say nothing / about my vagina
and nothing stays. Nothing stays
saying it.   Nothing vaginas.
Vaginas stay nothing. Nothing says
vaginas in the room.

I keep thinking I want to
fall in love with you but love
is so much constancy and.

I is so many words.

A CONGRESS OF BRING AND OF INVISIBLE:
THE LANGUAGE OF HEAVEN IS NO

city in which the body is disappearing.
city in which the aorist is resurrected.
city in which I cultivate disparation.
city in which the body permeates know.
city, you are rampant in the earlobes. a staple
furnished blithely in a tree.
city, you are Freudian in your constancy.
city, you are the permutation. of go.

—

city in which the feet stutter reckless.
city in which the vertigo is unnamed.
city in which the throat throws persimmon.
city in which the sheets are an impediment.
city in which I trouble you, like rain.
city in which the surface is disappearing.
city in which the manhole never leaves you.
city in which the visible is a treachery.
city in which her hair breaks, like shame.
city in which the whitewash is receding.
city in which the finally falls out.
in which the body is neither promise nor
kindness nor dare. city in which my back is newly token.

city in which the broken are uneven.
even and unbroken but still bound.

—

city in which your fists are a miracle.
city in which there remain 2 types of teeth.
city in which we revision a thankful girder.
city in which the violin is a fever.
a girder we must fashion from our teeth.
for the city in which the falling has already happened.
city in which the arm of every chair leads with *leave*.
city in which you protect things by erasing them.
city in which my tongue is frozen black.
city in which the brachial is unnerving.
city in which your hand is an opportunity.
city in which your hand defi(n)es my back.

—

city in which she will look hard and look harder and unsee me.
city in which I tend not to play music.
city in which I am desperate to become unseen.
city in which these hands are my hands when I hold you.
city in which *I love you* is a belt coming down.

city in which the cement arrived in us.
city in which smaller sounds prevail and I abuse them.
city in which my mother says *son*.
city in which there are 2 fingers. 2 fingers and no space in between.
arrive in us, contact, arrive.
city in which my mother says *you* to me.
city in which my father says *none*.

—

city in which I know nothing about the pressure a woman feels
depending on the placement of her knees.
city in which you were putting on your clothes.
city in which the ears were a cacophony.
city in which the wall, to both sides, is a necessity.
what now, with the insistence of hands. that they will
turn now and become a gift of flying things.
city in which we know the lungs are working
by the way the breath abandons the troubled mouth.

THE EXIT SIGNS ARE BEHIND US.

A hand laid down
on the draw of the back.

If I   you.

What happens when
we take away velcro
table skirts.

Give me yours.

Here is my ear.

BEG Approval

Because the only view we have is the one
that looks down on the knees. Praise perspective.
Praise shared disdain. Praise space made by connective
tissue; the synaptic cleft; elbowroom
at the dinner table; polite conversation;
lies you push through your teeth. Because dissecting
a dog's heart won't change the way it thinks. Praise redirected
traffic. Praise the gnarled lip that defends
the gentle bones. Because your mother was
a seahorse. And to think of her thin is
to empty all the ice from the tea glasses;
to strain the soup by driving it through your hand.
Praise tablecloths; sway-back chairs; the plastic
folds that protect slice after slice of cheese.

Because you never knew which way to fold
your napkin. Because the beginning
of most things feels so much like the end. Praise
the collapsed body of a dog licking
its genitals. Praise self sufficiency;
the snooze button; the sudden widening
of the bed when you hear your lover leave.
Praise surrender. Praise catch and release.
Because a shotgun blooms from the hunter's shoulder.
Praise the eardrum, the human skull found in Roque d'Aille
with the prosthetic seashell ear. Praise symmetry in all
things non-binary. Praise asexual reproduction.
Praise butch-bottoms and femme-tops. Praise
transistor radios. Praise scan and praise seek.

Because we seek confession it is transgressive
to name what lies between us. Because letting you go
is a trip to the mailbox. And to think of you
near is to prepare a picnic by slitting the paper bag,
then waiting for the groceries to run off the curb.
Praise the Heimlich maneuver; false advertising.
Praise the cellular mitosis you trust
is still occurring in the shower, in your memory,
at the bar. Praise the one bedroom we shared
on Mississippi; the softness of your forehead when you were sleeping.
Because the front door was always a semicolon.
Praise the darkness and finding you in it.
Praise inherent inequality; the objects
we pick from. Praise the objects we lose.

Praise losers who never knew the object
of the game. Because the laundromat is a bastion
of self-possession. Praise the mullet;
recessive genes; feathered hair. Praise self mutilation.
Because Mr. Faulk, my 8th grade science teacher,
was hit in the head by a baseball
and stuttered from that day on and was a champion
of the ethics of studying driver's ed. Praise empathy.
Praise assholes who brandish p.c. Because subdivision
occurs first in the occipital lobe of the brain. Because the leg-
lamp was a palindrome. Praise perma-grin;
rhetoric; the headache that prevents sex; the nap,
masturbation induced. Praise animosity between strangers.
Praise hormone therapy. Praise the color blue.

Had your mother not called me
into the bathroom with a bread knife
and tossed her foot up on the lip of the sink
as though it were a bar and she a rope,
I would not have stayed for dinner. Blueberry pie
notwithstanding. Knowing how blueberries expand
the capacity of memory in the brain. Praise Rubik's Cube.
Praise *Charlotte's Web*. Praise 2–5 years for rape.
Because my mother had a way of holding me
against my will. And to be loved by you
is to put a bumper sticker over the rearview
mirror that says something about road-kill.
Praise reverse. Praise me, disappearing
like a good daughter. Praise me, your only son.

Because gender is syntax, personified. Praise girl-boy
appetite. Praise resilient flesh. Praise paybacks.
Praise the wet towel rolled like a tongue
and snapped against your skin. Because strangers want nothing
more than to reveal you. Praise misrepresentation.
Praise the backhand that can testify
to the compliance of the face. Because purple hair
is a pig suit. Because drag racing is a double-
dipped cone. Because paralysis. Because horseshoes.
Because the answering machine. Because tone.
Praise *the ability to live in uncertainty and doubt*
without any irritable reaching after fact or reason.
Yeah, yeah. Pound, whatever.
Goddamned well of loneliness. *Make it new.*

Because Keats said something about *negative capability*
and now even our shoe size can be an in-between.
Because testimony can be stricken from the record.
Praise one-night stands; disposable dishrags;
the particulars of what we may seem. Praise selective hearing;
choosing this word (abort) instead of (miscarry)
that. Praise Hollywood. Praise the dog
chasing the tennis ball. Praise commitment;
self adhesive labels; the DNA your mother wore
and her mother before that; the tiny cuts
we give ourselves, hoping to spill out of our skin.
Because just yesterday the Earth was a bucket
and I filled it with toy guns. Praise playing dead.
Praise the view from above you as you fall to your knees.

GEPHYROMANIA

There is no person without a world.

Anne Carson

you may sleep in the corner (please: sweetly)

you may carry paper carry autumn in your mouth

Now that you are dead I can say this. Somehow I ended up with your hand towels. And I keep meaning to tell you we are teeming. (as in: across; as in: factor; as in: through) Needless to say I am hegemony. She is collared between forgiveness and rest.

Kissyface, give me your oxygen.
with what I wouldn't give for a buckshot
a Kodak. a catfish. a ground.

Like the light switches I spend hours (at)tending to. I feel as though I could write to you, 24 hours a day for 5 consecutive weeks, and still not touch you where you stand. You will never believe I am eating edamame. That this camera is digital. That the sound of my nevering is a pedigree. Accustomed in the fall of my back.

I barely understand your pelvis anymore. it is in someone else's living room and out of context. For a long second my hands are gently manacled. and I know you only in that cellular relief.

Leaning, as if on sound.

What we were promised was cornstarch.

Featuring I am all no and other miracles.

Elephants. Elephants out of days.

Who will I erase and in what company.

Who will shadow signature. Resist.

Suddenly Seymore and here's a fish in your hand.

What is behind me has been given sutures. (and rest.) (and rest.) (and sing.)

(and still)

I am not asking for that nearness. Nor even the possibility of reach. Please please this tempting terrible little enemy. discreet in our tissue and blessed.

I think I love you more with your derivative. for the camera you insisted I swallow. for the clean and crowded quiet little years. I would only admit this to you (dear blanky). To water, the body is still mostly land. (The hypothalamus remembers. The hypothalamus cares.)

I do not know anything about the periodic table and can therefore not speak to that. But. To say that the man wearing a 2-sizes-too-small yellow tarp beside the railroad tracks has "shit the bed" is a misrepresentation of a Monday. A deliberate obfuscation of the facts. You are a repetition, darling porch light, a repetitive. Suffering in the wake of my back.

Can someone please pass me

the Technicolor?

We left the oven on much more in that kitchen. Only the fact of what I was thinking there can separate me. Your hair breaks in and I am lovingly. Go little grass, burn back. Go little ween, kiss kiss.

we lay there for months
drawing back tiny muscle

and grafting an exegesis of skin

oddly in the middle you were a columbine. and the bees made a respite of your ears.

tonight, let's practice erosion.
it's finally my turn as the wind.

the cat door is cracked

I am certain. will you hold on

to me by dragging

our darling feet down

       what the mouth covers, and in covering, introduces.
we keep a tidy corridor of yesterday's when.

BRIDGES I AM THANKFUL
TO HAVE CROSSED

It was an act of thievery, but it was also an act of love.
—Eula Biss

Page 12 is for Miriam.

Page 13 owes a debt to Maureen Seaton's line, "Leaning, as if, on oil" from *Furious Cooking*.

"(ir)Retrieval"
> *Who are you when you are someone who's not been seen before?*
> *What are you when the thing you are does not yet have a name?*
> —Rebecca Brown

Sonnet 2 owes a debt to Jenny Boully, "It was called *You Fucking Suck* or *Perhaps It Was, After All, Because You Are Schizophrenic.*"

Sonnet 4 is a response to *Out* Magazine, April 2008, and is an ode to *Cocktails* by D.A. Powell.

Sonnet 7 is an ode to A F F.

"What Space Faith Can Occupy" was written for Kell and Jen. It takes as an epigraph a slightly altered line from Nicole Krauss' *History of Love: Once upon a time there was a girl who loved a girl and her laughter was a question she wanted to spend her whole life answering.*

"elegy" is for Miriam. and for me.

"On braiding hair already cut away from the scalp" is for Madeline.

"Tau(gh)t" is for Madeline.
> *In order for something to be handed over a hand must extend and a hand must receive.*
> —Claudia Rankine

> *How deep is the ocean?*
> *Enough to drown us all.*
> —Rebecca Brown

"Tau(gh)t" adapts a line from Eric Magrane's mirror poem. It also borrows a line ("Dear so and so...") from Richard Siken's poem "Litany in Which Certain Things Are Crossed Out."

"Misogyny is for people with mothers" was said to me by Amrit Donaldson. How could I not borrow that?

"Thaw" is for Ari. Stacy May Fowles wrote a brilliant essay, "Friction Burn," about being a straight woman engaged in BDSM relationships in *Nobody Passes*.

"territories of folding" is for my mother, Darline, and my sister, Julie.

"Crossing" is for Madeline.

"latitude: [perceived obsolescence]: unplanned" is for Miriam.

"The Palinode" is for Ari. It owes a debt to *Crush* by Richard Siken.

"On Minimalization" owes a debt to *Other Electricities* by Ander Monson.

"A Congress of Bring and Invisible: The Language of Heaven is No" is dedicated to the women of Invisible City. For what they allow to be seen.

Now that I am beyond the initial paralysis of calling one's first teachings into question, I am left with: be critical and sing.
   —C D Wright

"Beg Approval" is dedicated to Boyer Rickel. A master teacher. It was inspired, tonally, by *Dithyrambs* by Richard Katrovas.

Pages 86–87 are for Miriam.
   It wasn't so much that I was losing you, it was that I was losing the magical way in which you saw the world. It wasn't so much that I was mourning you, I was mourning the world.
   —Jenny Boully

Page 89 owes a debt to Kristi Maxwell's line, "tonight let's practice/erosion, it's my turn as weather," in *Realm Sixty-Four.*

BRIDGES OVER TROUBLED WATER

isabella/mamaw/mom/julie/nanaw and papaw/dad/tim/family/
movement salon/the architects/kristen/molly and charlie/jen and kell/kt/jenna/steph b/
stewball/josephine/darcee/rae rae/april/anna/kieran/deb and lynn/denise/
robin/melisa/outward bound/julia cameron/the indescribable A.T./
ian/lisa/hannah/julia and noah/frankie/court and jv/kate/
sam and sonny/katie k/jillian/amy s/crystal/cara b/bb/
femmes/bears/thinkers/trannyfags/radical queers/

richard jackson/maureen seaton/jane miller/
tenney nathanson/boyer rickel/casa libre/
matthea harvey/olga broumas/linda russo/
ca conrad/dawn lundy martin/joy ladin/
the editors of the drunken boat/the pinch/shampoo/
feminist formations/everyday genius/
trickhouse/volt/EOAGH/a trunk of delirium/jubilat/

lisa bowden and kore press/
tomiko jones/jeff clark/
janet holmes and ahsahta press/
stephen motika and nightboat books/

this is dedicated to mom and julie — long live the three musketeers

finally yous without finality: ari/miriam/madeline/
not less than, not greater than, three.

ABOUT THE AUTHOR

Hey y'all! My name is TC Tolbert (he/him/hey grrrl!) and I'm a Capricorn so I like walking up a mountain more than walking down; on the Enneagram, I'm a 1; learning is infinitely more interesting to me than knowing (and scarier, too); along with my partner, I am wildly blessed to get to care for two pit bulls who are willing to cuddle any time day or night; I am white and I was born and raised a girl in Hixson, TN as a speaking-in-tongues Pentecostal and I eventually came out as queer, feminist, anti-racist, and trans-masc; I now live in Tucson, which occupies the traditional territories of the Tohono O'odham and Pascua Yaqui peoples; I never cease to experience a simultaneous grief and deep love any time I pay attention to the world.

My publications include Gephyromania (originally published by Ahsahta Press in 2014, re-released by Nightboat Books in 2022), three chapbooks, one chaplet, and one micro-chap. I'm the co-editor (along with Trace Peterson) of Troubling the Line: Trans and Genderqueer Poetry and Poetics (Nightboat Books 2013). I was recently awarded an Academy of American Poets' Laureate Fellowship for my work with trans, non-binary, and queer folks as Tucson's Poet Laureate (2017-2020). I'm a certified Wilderness EMT and I spend my summers leading wilderness trips for Outward Bound. I practice Compositional Improvisation and thank this practice and my teachers for such a radically open way to be alive.

If you'd like to learn more about my writing, teaching, and/or collaborations, please visit www.tctolbert.com. I'm wild with gratitude for you, dear reader - your heart and your time.

NIGHTBOAT BOOKS

Nightboat Books, a nonprofit organization, seeks to develop audiences for writers whose work resists convention and transcends boundaries. We publish books rich with poignancy, intelligence, and risk. Please visit nightboat.org to learn about our titles and how you can support our future publications.

The following individuals have supported the publication of this book. We thank them for their generosity and commitment to the mission of Nightboat Books:

Anonymous (4)
Abraham Avnisan
Jean C. Ballantyne
The Robert C. Brooks Revocable Trust
Amanda Greenberger
Rachel Lithgow
Anne Marie Macari
Elizabeth Madans
Elizabeth Motika
Thomas Shardlow
Benjamin Taylor
Jerrie Whitfield & Richard Motika

This book is made possible, in part, by grants from the New York City Department of Cultural Affairs in partnership with the City Council and the New York State Council on the Arts Literature Program.